LET'S-READ-AND-FIND-OUT SCIENCE®

STAGE 1

From Seed to
PUMPKIN

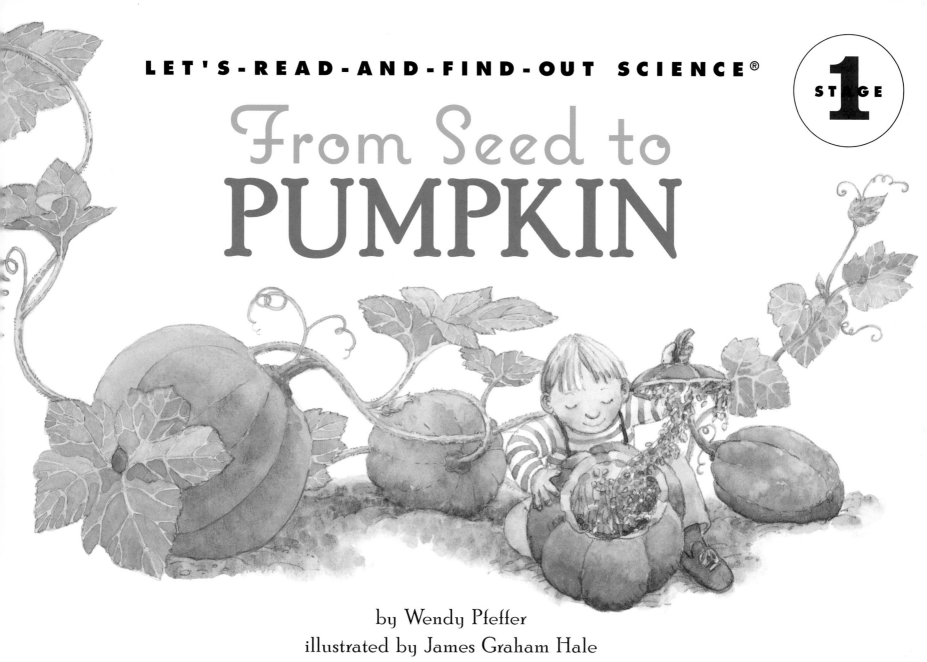

by Wendy Pfeffer

illustrated by James Graham Hale

HARPERCOLLINSPUBLISHERS

With thanks to Barbara J. Bromley,
Mercer County Horticulturist,
for sharing her vast knowledge of plants,
and with sincere appreciation to
Sarah Thomson for her valuable guidance

The *Let's-Read-and-Find-Out Science* book series was originated by Dr. Franklyn M. Branley, Astronomer Emeritus and former Chairman of the American Museum–Hayden Planetarium, and was formerly co-edited by him and Dr. Roma Gans, Professor Emeritus of Childhood Education, Teachers College, Columbia University. Text and illustrations for each of the books in the series are checked for accuracy by an expert in the relevant field. For more information about Let's-Read-and-Find-Out Science books, write to HarperCollins Children's Books, 10 East 53rd Street, New York, NY 10022, or visit our website at www.letsreadandfindout.com.

HarperCollins®, ☖ ®, and Let's Read-and-Find-Out Science® are trademarks of HarperCollins Publishers Inc.
From Seed to Pumpkin
Text copyright © 2004 by Wendy Pfeffer
Illustrations copyright © 2004 by James Graham Hale
Manufactured in China by South China Printing Company Ltd. All rights reserved.

Library of Congress Cataloging-in-Publication Data
Pfeffer, Wendy.
From seed to pumpkin / by Wendy Pfeffer ; illustrated by James Graham Hale.
p.   cm. — (Let's-read-and-find-out science. Stage 1)
ISBN 0-06-028038-7 — ISBN 0-06-028039-5 (lib. bdg.) — ISBN 0-06-445190-9 (pbk.)
1. Pumpkin—Life cycles—Juvenile literature.   [1. Pumpkin.]   I. Hale, James Graham, ill.   II. Title.
III. Series.
SB347.P44   2004   583'.63—dc21   00-054039

Typography by Elynn Cohen 12 13 SCP 20 19 18 17 16 15 14 ❖ First Edition

For Phil, Diane, Tim, and Jaime,
who grow all kinds of good food,
as well as great pumpkins
—W.P.

When spring winds warm the earth, a farmer plants hundreds of pumpkin seeds.

5

Every pumpkin seed can become a baby pumpkin plant.
Underground, covered with dark, moist soil, the baby plants
begin to grow.

As the plants get bigger, the seeds crack open. Stems sprout up. Roots dig down. Inside the roots are tubes. Water travels up these tubes the way juice goes up a straw.

In less than two weeks from planting time, green shoots poke up through the earth.

These shoots grow into tiny seedlings. Two leaves, called seed leaves, uncurl on each stem. They reach up toward the sun.

9

Sunlight gives these leaves energy to make food. Like us, plants need food to grow. But green plants do not eat food as we do. Their leaves make it.

To make food, plants need light, water, and air. Leaves catch the sunlight.

Roots soak up rainwater. And little openings in the leaves let air in. Using energy from the sun, the leaves mix the air with water from the soil to make sugar. This feeds the plant.

Soon broad, prickly leaves with jagged edges unfold on the stems.

The seed leaves dry up. Now the new leaves make food for the pumpkin plant.

Each pumpkin stem has many sets of tubes. One tube in each set takes water from the soil up to the leaves so they can make sugar.

The other tube in each set sends food back down so the pumpkin can grow.

14

The days grow warmer. The farmer tends the pumpkin patch to keep weeds out. Weeds take water from the soil. Pumpkin plants need that water to grow.

Pumpkin plants don't stand up tall. As the stems grow longer, they sprawl all over the ground. Before long, twisted, tangled vines cover the pumpkin patch.

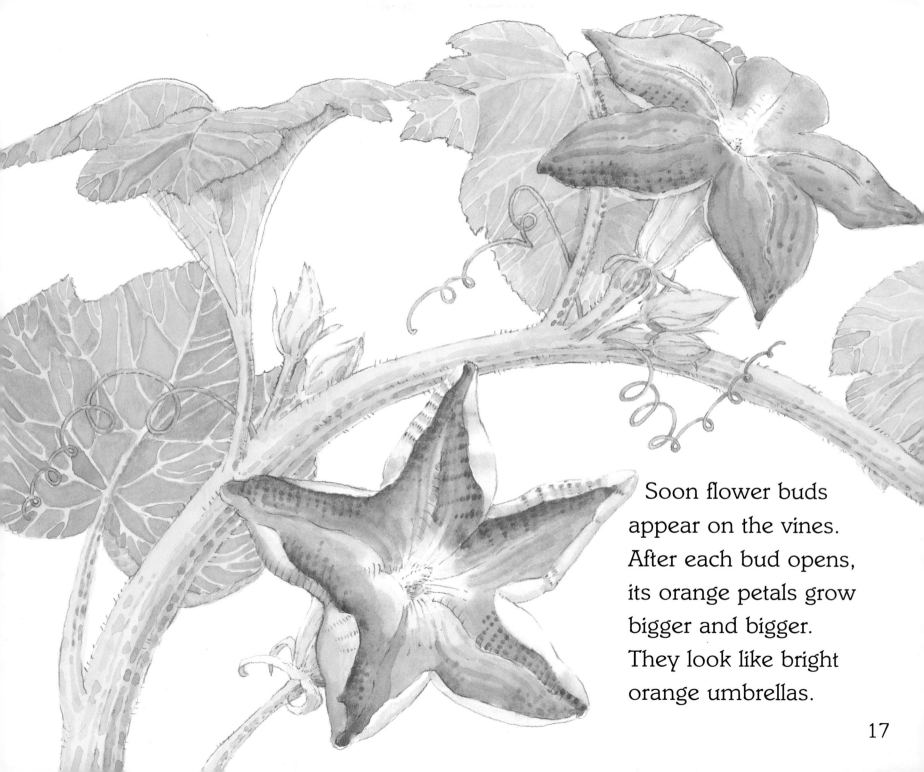

Soon flower buds
appear on the vines.
After each bud opens,
its orange petals grow
bigger and bigger.
They look like bright
orange umbrellas.

17

During the heat of the day, the flowers close.

18

They open again during the cool nights and early mornings. The bright orange flowers attract swarms of bees. The bees buzz about, carrying yellow pollen from the male flowers to the female flowers. Now pumpkins can grow.

The petals wither away. Where the flowers bloomed, tiny hard fruits begin to grow. Hundreds of these cling to the vines.

The days grow hot. All summer the warm sun and the cool rain help the tiny fruits grow larger and larger.

21

Soon summer is over. The cornstalks next to the pumpkin patch turn brown. Leaves on trees turn red, orange, and yellow.

Pumpkins change color, too. As they ripen, they change from green to yellow, then to orange.

In just four months small, flat, white pumpkin seeds have grown into big, fat, orange pumpkins.

24

The pumpkins are ripe and round, with lumps and bumps. They come in all sizes and shapes. And they're waiting in the autumn sun.

Some pumpkins will be carved into jack-o'-lanterns for Halloween.

Some will be baked into pumpkin pies for Thanksgiving.

Colorful leaves turn brown. Winter winds begin to blow, and soon the trees are bare. The farmer looks out over the pumpkin patch, where only a few dead vines remain.

But when spring winds warm the earth, once again he will plant hundreds of pumpkin seeds. And once again, they will grow—from seed to pumpkin.

FIND OUT MORE ABOUT PUMPKINS

- Did You Know a Pumpkin Is a Fruit?

The seed-bearing part of any flowering plant is called its fruit. Because a pumpkin has seeds in the middle it is really a fruit. Tomatoes, cucumbers, and pea pods are fruits, too. Because they are not sweet like other fruits we often call them vegetables.

- Roasted Pumpkin Seeds

When you carve your jack-o'-lantern, save the seeds you scoop out. Wash the pulp off. Then let them dry. Pumpkin seeds are filled with vitamins and minerals, so they are good to eat.

You will need:

1 cup of pumpkin seeds
paper towels
1/2 teaspoon salt

2 teaspoons cooking oil
mixing bowl
cookie sheet

1. Ask an adult to help.
2. Preheat oven to 350° F.
3. Wash seeds and pat dry between paper towels.
4. Mix seeds, salt, and cooking oil together in a bowl.
5. Spread mixture on cookie sheet.
6. Bake 15 minutes. Stir. Bake 15 minutes more.
7. Let them cool. Then enjoy the crispy golden treats.

• How Plants Drink Water

Pumpkin roots have tubes. They drink water from the ground the way you drink water with a straw. A celery stalk has tubes, too. They are also connected to roots, so the celery plant can drink water from the ground. You can see how the tubes in a stalk of celery work.

You will need:

several celery stalks
a sharp knife
red or blue food coloring
a glass, half full of water

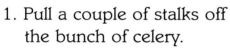

1. Pull a couple of stalks off the bunch of celery.
2. Ask an adult to help you cut them straight across the bottom.
3. Pour a few drops of red or blue coloring in the water and stir.
4. Place the celery stalks in the water with the cut ends down.
5. Wait about an hour.
6. See how the colored water has gone up the tubes in the celery.
7. Take one of the stalks of celery from the water and break it in half.
8. Look for the tubes now. See how the colored water has traveled up them.